OVERTHINKING ANTIDOTE

Cure your thoughts

BY

EMMY O. PARKA

TABLE OF CONTENTS

INTRODUCTION

OVERTHINKING, ALSO KNOWN AS RUMINATION, IS WHEN YOU REPEATEDLY CONCENTRATE ON THE SAME TOPIC OR SCENARIO TO THE POINT WHERE IT IMPAIRS YOUR LIFE. OVERTHINKING IS TYPICALLY CLASSIFIED INTO TWO TYPES: DWELLING ON THE PAST AND FRETTING ABOUT THE FUTURE.

YOU MAY FEEL "STUCK" OR UNABLE TO TAKE ANY ACTION IF YOU STRUGGLE WITH OVERTHINKING. IT CAN BE DIFFICULT TO CLEAR YOUR MIND

AND CONCENTRATE ON ANYTHING ELSE.

WHILE STRESS CAN BE CAUSED BY OVERTHINKING, NOT ALL TENSION IS NEGATIVE. HAVING A LOT OF THOUGHTS ABOUT A DIFFICULT CIRCUMSTANCE CAN MOTIVATE YOU TO ACT IN THE SHORT TERM.

WHEN YOU'RE APPREHENSIVE ABOUT A BIG WORK PRESENTATION, FOR EXAMPLE, THAT STRESS CAN HELP YOU GET MOVING.

IT MAY FORCE YOU TO WORK HARD ON THE PROJECT AND ARRIVE AT WORK EARLY ON THE DAY OF THE

PRESENTATION TO ENSURE YOU ARE ON TIME. OVERTHINKING CAN ALSO PROVIDE INSIGHT INTO YOUR VALUES AND POTENTIAL OPPORTUNITIES FOR PERSONAL GROWTH.

"NOT ALL OVERTHINKING IS BAD," ARGUES FOLEY. HOWEVER, IT BECOMES PROBLEMATIC WHEN IT INHIBITS YOUR ABILITY TO ACT OR INTERFERES WITH YOUR DAILY LIFE AND WELL-BEING.

CHAPTER 1
REASON
WHY
PEOPLE OVERTHINKING WHEN STRESS AND WORRY

Stress and worry are the two most common causes of overthinking. Aside from these two, low self-esteem and self-doubt are major causes of overthinking. In addition to highlighting the pandemic condition, social isolation has caused us tension and anxiety, and anxiety is a natural response to dread.

Overthinking is one of the most common causes of worry, irritation, and stress.

Whether it's worrying about the future, ruminating on the past, or being too judgmental of others, our ability to think critically is a two-edged sword that we'd all do well to be more cautious with. But, before you try to quit overthinking, it's a good idea to understand why you overthink in the first place.

As a psychologist, I've seen the seven causes listed below over and over again among patients who deal with overthinking.

But, before you try to quit overthinking, it's a good idea to understand why you overthink in the first place.

As a psychologist, I've seen the seven causes listed below over and over again among patients who deal with overthinking.

You've probably had restless nights when your brain just won't shut off, whether you're a chronic overthinking or you need to make a difficult decision. It happens to all of us at some point in our life; we all encounter occurrences that lead us to be concerned or stressed. While it's natural to think things through while making a decision or evaluating a situation, overthinking occurs when you can't get out of your own head.

The classic meaning of overthinking is "to think about something too much or for too long." So, when does thinking cross the line into overthinking? It's when you can't seem to turn off your worries. When you pose too much, you get stuck, unable to make a decision or take action.

5 REASONS OF OVERTHINKING

1. **worry about the future and the past:** Overthinking may appear as rumination in many circumstances, which entails ruminating over events from the past or even the present with a negative perspective. There are constructive strategies to reframe your ideas and stress less, whether your inclination to overthink leads you into the past or focuses on the future.

2. **letting negativity build up in your mind:**

Negative thinking impairs your brain's ability to comprehend, think, and build memories. Chronic stress can be caused by negative attitudes and emotions of helplessness and hopelessness, which disrupt the body's hormone balance, deplete the brain chemicals essential for happiness, and affect the immune system.

3. **feeling depressed or stressed:** Both can have similar effects on you, yet there are significant variances. Depression symptoms might be much more severe. They are good for at least two weeks. Depression causes severe changes

in mood, such as painful sadness and despair.

4. **having "over-analyzing:**
Overthinking and over-analysis are frequently motivated by fear - fear of making a mistake, fear of missing out, or fear of losing money. These anxieties might cause an endless loop of analysis in which you constantly second-guess your judgments and struggle to take action.

5. **Stress and anxiety:**
Stress causes both mental and physical symptoms, including annoyance, rage, exhaustion,

muscle pain, digestive problems, and difficulties sleeping. Anxiety, on the other hand, is characterized by continuous, excessive worry that persists even in the absence of a stressor.

CHAPTER 2
SIDE EFFECTS OF

OVERTHINKING

- Fatigue.
- Headaches.
- Nausea.
- Difficulty concentrating.
- Trouble sleeping.
- Changes in appetite.

Fatigue: Thinking causes your brain to expend a large amount of energy. Your brain is in charge of directing your body's activities, processing sensory information, and making decisions.

Headaches: A headache can occur when your body is depleted of nutrients and hydration. Uncorrected eyesight defects: Eye strain can result in a headache.

Nausea: Your heart rate quickens and your breathing rate quickens. You might also feel a little queasy. You can feel a little nauseated during a period of intense worry.

Difficulty Concentrating: A person may have to expend more energy to focus on something other than their concern. They may believe that their nervous thoughts are continuously interfering with their mental processes. This can make it difficult to concentrate and think coherently.

Trouble Sleeping: Because negative ideas are frequently intellectually stimulating, dwelling on them might exacerbate sleeplessness. It's worth noting that in one study, people who were forced to focus on their regrets before bedtime took longer to fall asleep than those who weren't.

Changes In Appetite: Anxiety can cause a loss of appetite or an increase in appetite. These effects are primarily due to hormonal changes in the body, but some people may also avoid eating as a result of the physical sensations of anxiety.

Top 10 Damaging Effects Of Overthinking On Your Mental And Physical Health

1. **Anxiety:** Anxiety is a sensation of tension, concerned thoughts, and physical changes such as elevated blood pressure. Anxiety disorders are characterized by repeated intrusive thoughts or concerns. They may avoid specific situations due to anxiety. From butterflies in your stomach to a racing heart, emotions can run the gamut. You may feel out of control as if there is a schism between your mind and body

You may be afraid of something in general, or you may be afraid of a specific location or event. You may have a panic attack in some instances

Symptoms Anxiety sources that can be trusted include:

difficult-to-control worrisome thoughts or beliefs restlessness difficulties with concentration weariness from falling asleep irritability unidentified aches and pains

Your anxiety symptoms may differ from those of others. That is why it is critical to understand how anxiety manifests itself.

2. **Depression**: Depression (major depressive disorder) is a widespread and significant medical ailment that has a negative impact on how you feel, think, and act. It is, thankfully, treatable. Depression creates feelings of melancholy and/or a loss of interest in previously appreciated activities. It can cause a number of mental and physical problems, as well as a reduction in your capacity to operate at work and at home.

Depression symptoms can range from moderate   to severe and include the following:

Sadness or a gloomy mood

Loss of interest or pleasure in previously appreciated activities

Appetite changes — weight loss or increase unrelated to diets

Sleeping difficulties or excessive sleep

Energy loss or increased weariness

Increase in meaningless physical activity (for example, inability to sit still, pacing, handwringing) or delayed motions or speech (these activities must be severe enough for others to notice)

Feeling insignificant or sorry

Problems thinking, concentrating, or making decisions

Suicide or death thoughts

3. **Insomnia**: The majority of cases of insomnia are caused by poor sleeping habits, sadness, anxiety, a lack of exercise, a chronic ailment, or a specific prescription. Symptoms may include trouble falling or staying asleep, as well as a lack of sleep.
Insomnia treatment includes modifying sleep habits, behavioral therapy, and identifying and treating underlying problems. Sleeping medications can also be utilized, but the negative effects should be closely watched.

Maintain a consistent sleep routine. Maintain a consistent bedtime and waking time from day to day, including on weekends.

Maintain your level of activity...

Examine your meds...

Naps should be avoided or limited.

Caffeine and alcohol should be avoided or limited, and nicotine should be avoided.

Don't put up with suffering.

Large meals and alcohol should be avoided before going to bed.

4. **Paralysis**: Strokes are the most common cause of paralysis, and

they are usually caused by a blocked artery in your neck or brain.

It can also be caused by damage to your brain or spinal cord, such as in a car accident or sports injury.

Paralysis signs and symptoms

You are unable to move any part of your face or body.

Your face or body is frail or saggy.

Your face or body is always numb, uncomfortable, or tingly.

Muscle spasms and twitches make your face or body stiff.

5. **You could live less time**: The medical school compared the brains of people aged 60 to 100 and beyond and found that the younger group had lower amounts of protein linked to calming down activity.

The brain works too hard while thinking too much, depleting its protein supply. However, overusing your brain might have unanticipated repercussions that you might not have anticipated.

6. **Unbalanced chemical composition of the body**: According to the chemical imbalance theory, depression is caused by changes in neurotransmitter levels in the brain. The effectiveness of antidepressant drugs is the most commonly utilized evidence to support the chemical imbalance argument.

A chemical imbalance in the brain can impair the emotional, memory, and sensation systems. Although overthinking will not cause permanent brain damage, everything you do and think has an effect on your body.

7. **The appetite varies**: When you have a decreased appetite, you have a decreased desire to eat. It is also known as a loss of appetite or a bad appetite. Anorexia is the medical name for this. A wide range of illnesses can induce a decline in appetite. These include both mental and physical disorders.

Anxiety causes emotional and psychological changes in your

body to assist you in dealing with the stress. These changes frequently influence the stomach and digestive tract, causing you to lose your appetite. If you're stressed, your hunger will normally return once you're less stressed.

8. **Creativity lost**: Overthinking is a killer of creativity. According to science, both analysis and creativity occur in the prefrontal cortex of our brains. This means that focusing too much on

analysis depletes the brain power available for creativity. Worry and self-doubt feel heavy, confining, and limiting.

9. **Social competencies are impacted**: Social competence entails the ability to assess social situations and understand what is expected or required; to recognize the sentiments and intentions of others; and to choose the most suitable social behaviors for the given setting.

10. You have a higher risk of developing mental diseases: Overthinking is not a medical illness, although it can be a symptom of sadness or anxiety. According to Duke, overthinking is frequently connected with generalized anxiety disorder (GAD). GAD is distinguished by an excessive concern about a variety of issues.

What you can do to overcome your overthinking

If you notice yourself overthinking, there are steps you can take to limit your worrying and cope in a healthier way, says Duke.
If you struggle to turn off your thoughts at night or if your overthinking is interfering with or affecting your daily life, talking to your doctor or a therapist can help. "The most effective treatment is cognitive behavioral therapy," says Duke. Your therapist will work with you to challenge your negative thoughts and develop coping skills that can help alleviate your worry.

Duke also says that positive coping strategies like meditation, reading, or writing down your worries can help lessen your anxiety.

It's also important to make sure you have adequate social support and that you're resisting the urge to keep things inside. And don't forget about engaging in healthy habits like eating a well-balanced diet and exercising.

"Pay attention to how much caffeine or alcohol you consume, as these can increase anxiety," cautions Duke. "Also, try to avoid having too little or too much downtime and engaging in a lot of social media or news consumption, as these things are also going to feed anxiety.

CHAPTER 3
CATEGORIES OF OVERTHINKING

Overthinking is classified into two types: rumination (rehashing past experiences) and worrying (hyperfocusing on an anxious anxiety about the future).

Quotes About What Overthinking Is Like When You Have Anxiety

- "I'm always overthinking the future, and all the things that could go wrong."

- "When I'm out with people - especially people I don't know - I overthink the smallest things like what people will think of my tone of voice, my body language, what I'm wearing, and of course what I say."

- "It's so debilitating ... it's overwhelming to make a decision about even little things like where to go for lunch or what to wear."

- "Anxiety makes it so hard to let go of things. Whether it's a mistake I made in the past that I keep overthinking or a joke someone made today that I worry there's some hidden meaning behind ... it's hard to just accept things for what they are and move forward."

- "I'm constantly overthinking the worst possible outcome and how I can prevent it from happening. Like if I have a presentation at work, let's say - I'll rehearse every possible aspect of it so that I (hopefully) don't end up embarrassed."

- "For me, my overthinking gets activated anytime something is "unknown". Last night, for example, I was planning to go out with some friends, and then three hours before we were due to meet, two of them decided to change the restaurant. It sent me into overdrive thinking about where I'd park, what the layout of the restaurant would be, what I would order, and how far it would be from the table to the bathroom in case I felt panicked and needed to re-compose myself. These are all things I really like to know in advance because when I don't, it can lead to a panic attack."

- "I can't take anything at face value - everything needs to be dissected and analyzed. My mind spirals thinking - is there any hidden detail that I may be missing? Is there anything that I may not be understanding? What if this? What if that? It's absolutely exhausting and sucks the fun out of everything."

- "The number one thing I overthink is: I wonder if people actually like me, or if they're just pretending?"

- "I judge myself for the small situations that cause me to panic. I question how I'll be able to thrive if I'm so sensitive and fragile."

- "I overthink and worry that my anxiety will push people away and that they'll leave me. This has consumed countless hours of my time."

- "I doubt my capabilities. What if I don't have what it takes? What if I crumble under the pressure? What if I can't live up to the expectations others have of me? I have zero control over these thoughts."

- "Anytime I say something, I get scared I'll be judged for it or be misunderstood. I'm constantly

thinking about how to filter myself
and not stuff up."

- "Every time I feel the slightest bit
  unwell, I start thinking and
  panicking that I've got a serious
  illness. I get consumed with
  thoughts like, am I going to die? If I
  die, then who'll take care of my
  children? What the hell is going to
  happen to them? These are the
  thoughts my mind turns to and
  focuses on until I see a doctor -
  who, the last time I went, told me
  the reason my stomach was sore was
  because I'd been eating too much
  acidic fruit."

- "I am always thinking of anything
  that may catch me by surprise or off

guard. My biggest fear is freezing up."

- **"What if I make a mistake?** What if I make the wrong decision? What's going to happen then? What will the consequences be? These are the kind of thoughts that plague me every time I have to do something or make a choice."

Quotes About What Overthinking Is Like When You Have Depression

- "I get stuck on something that happened in the past, and go through it in my mind over and over and over again."

- "I overthink all the mistakes that I've made ... it's like depression is trying to gather evidence for why I should hate myself."

- "Overthinking makes simple tasks turn into the biggest things ever. Before having a shower in the morning for example, I'll sometimes question if I have the energy for it ... then I'll wonder how I'll be able to get through the day if it's a struggle to even find enough energy to shower ... then I'll feel discouraged and unmotivated ... then I'll feel trapped because I know I'll have the same struggle tomorrow. It's exhausting."

- "I overthink the purpose of day-to-day life. What's the point of this? Why do I bother with that?

Everything is challenged and questioned."

- "Whenever I do the smallest thing wrong, I beat myself up about it for days. I can't stop replaying it and criticizing myself for it."

- "I'm constantly comparing myself to others - where we're at in life, what they're doing and what I'm not, how easy some things are for them that are hard for me, etcetera. It feeds into me feeling worthless and like I'm always falling short."

- "I continuously question why I can't just be 'normal' ... it feels like everything I do is wrong so I'm constantly critiquing myself."

- "I'm looking for any reason to have hope for a better future. I feel like I'm always trying to catch up but am always behind."

- "I keep thinking about how much depression has taken from me and is holding me back from things. Sometimes I get so consumed with anger that it's hard to focus on anything else."

- "It's the 'I'll never' when depression hits - the 'I'll never amount to anything' ... 'I'll never achieve my goals' ... 'I'll never get better ...'"

- "My thoughts start spiraling the moment depression makes things harder than I think they should be - like trying to read or focusing on a work project, for example. I get overwhelmed easily and then start putting myself down."

- "I overthink the most when I'm numb and can't find any meaning in the world. I question 'Is this all there is? Will things always be this way?' It's like I'm trying to find hope."

- "I go through waves where I can't feel anything ... where nothing brings me joy or makes me feel alive. I ruminate about this and whether I'll ever feel like 'me' again."

Quotes About What Overthinking Is When It Comes To A Relationship

- "I read into the smallest of things - the smallest changes in my partner's behaviors or their mood. It's like my brain goes into overdrive trying to find every possible explanation for every little thing (usually thinking the worst every time)."

- "Even when things are good, I still find ways to overthink - about whether it'll last, about the future, and about whether things are ACTUALLY good."

- "I overthink whether they actually love me. Even though they show me and tell me they do, it's like a part of me just refuses to believe it."

- "For me, it's the worst-case scenario I fear the most. I overthink anything that may even slightly suggest they could happen."

- "I overthink what to say and how to act. It's like I can't just be myself and do what feels natural."

- "If my partner ever needs alone time or wants to do something without me, I always think it's because I've done something wrong or because they must be sick of me (even though I know it's natural to want some space and independence in a relationship)."

- "I struggle to trust my partner after being cheated on in the past, and I can't help but look for any sign that they may be hiding something from me because I'm scared of getting hurt again."

- "I worry whether this is the right relationship for me. I put so much pressure on it and am constantly evaluating it - to the point that at times, I know I'm sucking the fun out of it."

- "I always worry if my partner is happy and question whether I'm enough for them. Do I make them happy enough? Are they actually happy in our relationship?"

- "I overthink our small disagreements so much ... I worry that they're the unraveling of us and if they'll lead to us breaking up."

- "I over-read text messages like crazy. I obsessively worry why someone may be taking a little longer to reply than usual and catastrophize the reason for it. Other times I panic about why they did/didn't use a particular emoji."

- "My brain goes into overdrive whenever my boyfriend goes quiet. I wonder what he's thinking about and get carried away playing out all sorts of worst-case scenarios."

- "Whenever they have something on that doesn't include me, I personalize it and think they are avoiding me. Then I start worrying about our future and questioning things."

- "When things start becoming more intimate with someone or I start letting my guard down, I get anxious and start overthinking everything that could go wrong."

Quotes About What Overthinking Is Like At Night Time

- "I just lie in bed awake when I should be sleeping, thinking about everything that's wrong with my life. It feels impossible to shut off my mind."

- "The dread for tomorrow sets in at night - thinking about all the things I'll have to do that I wish I could avoid."

- "I get anxious about going to sleep and start thinking about whether I definitely locked the front door, if the stove is off, etcetera."

- "I replay the events of the day as if to check whether everything went OK. I then zero in on any mistake I made and think how I could correct it."

- "Sometimes, I'll just remember some random awkward incident that happened years ago where I embarrassed myself, and start replaying it over and over again in my mind."

- "For me, I get lost in my imagination and a life that is a total escape from the one I'm living. Then I start second-guessing everything."

- "I always go back to whether I'm on the right career path. I don't feel fulfilled, and worry whether it'll always be like this and whether I should've chosen the path that makes me happier."

- "It takes me ages to fall asleep at night, and the longer it takes, the more I start overthinking the next day - about how much more tired I'll be, and about how much more difficult it will now be to function."

- "When I'm lying in bed all by myself, I sometimes find myself thinking: what if I never meet my person? What if no one will ever love me? What if I die alone?"

- "I question whether I'm doing enough with my life. I feel like I'm wasting it and missing out on things."

- "Just before I fall asleep is when my biggest worries surface. Sometimes it's money-related, and other times it's about my relationship. Whatever it is just comes up when I'm in bed and then my thoughts start spiraling."

- "After another day and its challenges, I wonder whether there'll ever be a time when I feel on top of things - where I'll be flowing, confident, and really in control of my life."

* "In the dark of night, I have a habit of shaming myself for things like eating too much at dinner or sending an email that I didn't work well enough. It's like my brain's nightly ritual to find fault in everything from that day."

Quotes About How Hard It Is To Stop Overthinking

* "Once a big fear gets triggered like 'they're going to leave me', my anxiety just completely takes over and no logic can bring it back in."

* "I know overthinking sabotages me in so many situations, but it's so hard to shut my mind off and make it stop. It just becomes too loud to ignore."

- "It's like I'm playing whack-a-mole with the 'what ifs' that are constantly popping up. No matter how hard I try to squash them, more and more keep appearing."

- "As much as I want to be present and live in the moment, I can't seem to let go of everything else. I feel like the moment I do, bad things will happen so I must always keep analyzing things."

- "Overthinking is like walking on a tight-rope - it's like I need to think about everything to feel in control, but it always runs the risk of going too far which makes me feel less and less in control."

- "For me, any attempt to stop overthinking just leads to more and more overthinking."

- "Stopping overthinking feels like driving a car with no breaks. I keep desperately trying to slam them but nothing works."

- "I crave an escape from my brain. I feel powerless because any attempt to dial things in and feel a sense of order falls short."

- "It's hard to stop overthinking because I feel like I need to run through every option to put myself at ease."

- "Overthinking is like an addiction. I feel like my brain is addicted to thinking, and it's only getting more rapid and intense with time ... like I'm getting more and more stuck in my head."

CBT & DBT Strategies To Help You Stop Overthinking

If you struggle with overthinking, then as the above quotes touch upon - and as you can likely relate to yourself - it can lead to a variety of consequences, including:

- Stress;

- Relationship conflict;

- Difficulty sleeping, feeling exhausted, and struggling to function the next day as a result;

- Difficulty concentrating (as overthinking can make it really hard to focus on anything that's taking place outside of your head);

- Increased severity of depression and anxiety.

And, for this reason, now that we've looked at the nine different types of overthinking as well as 50+ quotes about what overthinking is like, the next thing we'd like to do in this blog post is share with you three cognitive behavioral therapy and dialectical behavior therapy strategies to help you stop overthinking.

Distinguish Between PRODUCTIVE vs

UNPRODUCTIVE Worry In Order To Stop Overthinking

"Productive worry" is worry over something which you have control over. The reason why this kind of worrying can be considered "productive" is because it's *problem-solving-orientated* in nature, and consequently, it can lead to you developing a plan of action to help you prevent what you're worried about from actually happening.

On the other hand, however, "unproductive worry" is worry over something which you *don't* have control over. The reason why this kind of worrying can be considered "unproductive" is because since you have no control over the outcome you fear, then it isn't problem-solving-orientated in nature. As a result, it has no beneficial purpose, and all it's doing is fueling the negative consequences of overthinking that we mentioned above.

For this reason, it can be really, *really* helpful to pinpoint which components of your worrying thoughts you have some control over.

And, to see how you can do this in practice, let's take a look at the example worrying thought "If _________ gets elected, they may decrease jobs in my industry, which means that I may lose my job, and if that were to happen, then it would significantly compromise my ability to support my family."

- **<u>Component 1</u>:** Aside from casting your vote for your preferred party and/or candidate, you most likely have no control over the election outcome. For this reason, worrying over whether or not _______ gets elected would be considered "unproductive worry".

- **<u>Component 2</u>:** In this case, if you do get elected, you may be able to join a protest or lobby the government in some way to try to convince them not to implement this policy change. However, on an individual level, you're unlikely to have much control over what policies the government chooses to implement, and for this reason, worrying about whether or not _______ will decrease jobs in your industry if they're elected would be considered "unproductive worry".

. **<u>Component 3:</u>** this means that I may lose my job Now, this is something that you may have at least *some* control over. After all, the more valuable of an employee you are, the less likely you are to lose your job – right? So, if you do everything in your power to make yourself as indispensable to your company as possible, then you may be able to decrease the probability of losing your job. For this reason, worrying about what you can do to make yourself as indispensable to your company as possible in order to minimize the probability of you losing your job would be considered "productive worry".

- **<u>Component 4:</u>** if [losing your job] does happen, then it would significantly compromise my ability to support my family. Once again, this is something else you have some control over – since your income from your current job is not the only method you have of supporting your family. Consequently, worrying about how you would support your family if you did lose your job would also be considered "productive worry".

So, out of the four components of this worrying thought, we've identified two components of it that you exercise at least some degree of control over:

1. The probability of you losing your job;

2. Your ability to support your family if you do.

What To Do About The Components Of Your Worry That You Have Some Control Over

For those components of your worry that you have some control over, we encourage you to make

an action plan that details the steps you need to follow to try to prevent what you're worried about from actually happening.

Now, in our example, what you want to avoid happening is firstly, losing your job, and secondly, being unable to support your family if you do lose your job. So, with these objectives in mind, let's create an example action plan of how you could achieve them.

ACTION PLAN #1: To Try To Achieve The Objective Of Not Losing Your Job

Like we said before, this in all likelihood is best achieved by trying to make yourself as valuable and indispensable to your employer or company as you can possibly be – so that if job cuts do end up happening, you may be more likely than other people to keep your job. An example action plan that you could follow to try to do this may be:

1. Making a commitment to yourself to being the hardest working person on your team;

2. Doing the "dirty work" that other team members don't want to do;

3. Taking only half your lunch hour so that you can be more productive;

4. Take the initiative to do whatever you can to make your boss's life easier.

ACTION PLAN 2: To Try To Achieve The Objective Of Still Being Able To Support Your Family Even If You Do Lose Your Job

Luckily, the policy you're worried about being implemented which could affect your job is unlikely to be enacted the week ________ is elected into power (if they are in fact elected, and if they do in fact go ahead with implementing this policy). Consequently, you still have time to try to save as much money as possible – which, in the worst-case scenario where you do lose your job, would help keep you and your family afloat until you can find a new job. In this case, an example action plan to help you save money may look like:

1. Until you have more job certainty, reduce your and your family's expenses on items A, B, C, and D – since they are not 100% essential, and you could manage to go without them for a while.

2. Picking up flexible work (as an Uber driver for example) for 10 hours a week to help you make some supplementary income on top of your current income. A

flexible job like this may also be one you could transition to full-time if you do lose your job – at least until you're able to find work in your industry again.

The Power Of Following Your Action Plan

Of course, it goes without saying that after making your action plan, it's important that you follow it – so that you actually minimize the probability of your future worry occurring. Additionally:

1. The mere act of following your action plan and taking proactive steps to try to control your life for the better is – regardless of the outcome – likely to make

you feel more confident and empowered, as opposed to feeling hopeless, stressed out, anxious, and/or depressed.

2. Not only that but keeping busy by following your action plan can also help prevent you from idly ruminating on your worrying thoughts – which is another important reason why following your action plan can help worrying thoughts from raging war on your mental health.

What To Do About The Components Of Your Worrying Thoughts That You <u>Don't</u> Have Any Control Over

When it comes to unproductive worry, then rather than continuing to engage with it and engage with it, we really encourage you to instead try to □ *let go of it.*

In practice, you could do this by, for example:

- Distracting yourself - such as by watching television, listening to music, or calling up a friend and talking to them.

- Doing the 5-4-3-2-1 mindfulness exercise (which is the first exercise we share in our blog post titled <u>3 DBT Mindfulness Exercises For Depression, Anxiety & PTSD</u>).

- Doing a thought delusion exercise (that we'll share with you below).

- Doing something to soothe your senses – such as by smelling a scented candle, listening to the sounds of nature, or stroking something soft.

- Exercising – such as going for a run through the park, lifting weights at the gym, or walking up and down your street.

- Visualizing yourself somewhere safe, calm, and peaceful – such as lying on a sandy beach; or amidst rolling, lush green hills in the country.

- Thinking about something funny – such as a hilarious memory or a scene from your favorite comedy show.

- Recalling a pleasant memory from the past and allowing it to uplift you – such as from your favorite vacation or the day your child was born, example.

Practicing Mindfulness To Stop Overthinking

The second strategy we'd like to share with you to help you stop overthinking is to ☐ *practice mindfulness* ☐ - which in case you don't know, involves anchoring yourself to the present moment and focusing on nothing more than the here and now. For example:

- If you're practicing mindfulness while you eat – i.e. "eating mindfully" – then it could take the form of, for example, focusing on how each mouthful of food tastes, how its texture changes as you chew it, and what it feels like going down your throat.

- If you're practicing mindfulness while you shower – i.e. "showering mindfully" – then it could take the form of, for example, focusing on how the water feels crashing down on your skin, the scent of the soap you're using, and what it's like lathering it all over your body.

- If you're practicing mindfulness while you're drawing – i.e. "mindful drawing" – then it would take the form of focusing 100% of your attention on your drawing (as opposed to, for example, watching television at the same time, being distracted by your phone constantly buzzing, and/or thinking about something else that's unrelated to your drawing).

Practicing mindfulness in this way can help you stop overthinking, because

it can help you prevent intrusive, negative, and/or worrying thoughts from creeping into the present moment, and help prevent you from engaging in rumination about the past. After all, when you're living in the present moment, then by definition, you're experiencing life as it is *right now.* Therefore (also by definition), for example:

- You aren't worrying about the future (because you're focused on the present);

- You aren't ruminating about the past (because you're focused on the present);

- You aren't constantly overthinking about anything else that isn't related to the present.

Examples Of Practicing Mindfulness Throughout Your Day

Since mindfulness simply involves centering your attention on the present moment, it can be practiced anywhere, anytime. And, to give you a couple of examples of how you could go about your day more mindfully, below, we'd like to expand upon two examples we touched on above *mindful eating* and *mindful showering*.

• **Mindful Eating**

Once you've found a peaceful place to sit, set your meal in front of you. Before you take your first bite, take a moment to think about the food you're going to eat. Focus on the way your food looks. What are its colors? What shapes does it take? Focus on the way your food smells. How would you describe it? Focus on the way your food feels. What kind of texture does it have? Is it soft? Is it solid? If it's a sandwich for example, how does it feel to hold it? If it's soup, how does it feel to lift up a spoonful? Finally, focus on the way it will taste. As you bring the first bite towards your mouth, anticipate it. How does your body react? What sensations do you feel? Where do you feel them? Next, take your first bite. Chew your food slowly. What is its temperature like? What flavors stand out to you? What is your favorite aspect of your food? Also, notice how it stimulates your other senses and body parts. For example, if it's crunchy, you might feel it in your ears. If it's spicy, you might feel it on your lips. Then, notice how the texture of your food changes as you chew it, and finally, concentrate on the sensation of swallowing. How does it feel going down your throat? Eat each and every bite this way — mindfully — until you finish your meal.

- **Mindful Showering**

Just like with mindful eating, when you're having a shower, try to be as present in the moment as possible. Start by focusing on how the water feels against your skin. Is it warm or cool? How about the water pressure? Is it strong, gentle, or somewhere in between? What does the soap feel like? Is it smooth or gritty? Does it lather when it makes contact with your body? How does your shampoo smell? And, how does it make you feel? For example, as you massage it into your scalp, do you begin to feel more wakeful? Or, does it make you sleepy? Just as with mindful eating, take your time with this exercise. Clean yourself thoroughly and savor the experience. Any time you catch your mind wandering, just return your thoughts to the present moment in the shower and refocus on the water hitting your body, the soap gliding over your skin, and the other ways that your five senses are being stimulated. Do this for the entire duration of your shower before toweling yourself off.

☐ Final Words On Mindfulness When It Comes To Overthinking

Regardless of what it is you're doing throughout your day – whether eating, showering, or anything else – then like we've been saying, you can do it mindfully by just focusing wholly on whatever it is that you're doing. And, the more and more you get accustomed to mindfully going about your day, the less and less likely you are to overthink anything that's unrelated to the present moment.

Practicing Thought Diffusion To Stop Overthinking

Thought diffusion is a technique that's popular in dialectical behavior the ropy and one that you can implement to help you detach from your intrusive, ruminative, and/or worrying thoughts and gain some separation from them - as opposed to continuing to overthink and overthink.

For this strategy, we encourage you to start by closing your eyes, taking a few deep breaths, and then, trying to imagine your thoughts as something that is harmlessly drifting away from you. For example:

- Imagine that each of your thoughts is a balloon, floating away in the sky;

- Imagine that you're standing at the top of a hill or a sloping street and that your thoughts are tennis balls rolling down it;

- Imagine that you're at the beach and that your thoughts are birds flying by in the distance;

- Imagine yourself sitting on a street-side bench, and that your thoughts are cars passing by in front of you.

If you prefer another form of imagery that captures your thoughts coming and going like so, then of course, you're most welcome to use that. Either way, just visualize your thoughts as being outside of your head, floating away, rolling away, passing you by, etcetera, without trying to analyze them, without trying to judge them, without trying to suppress them, without trying to overthink them, and without trying to buy into them.

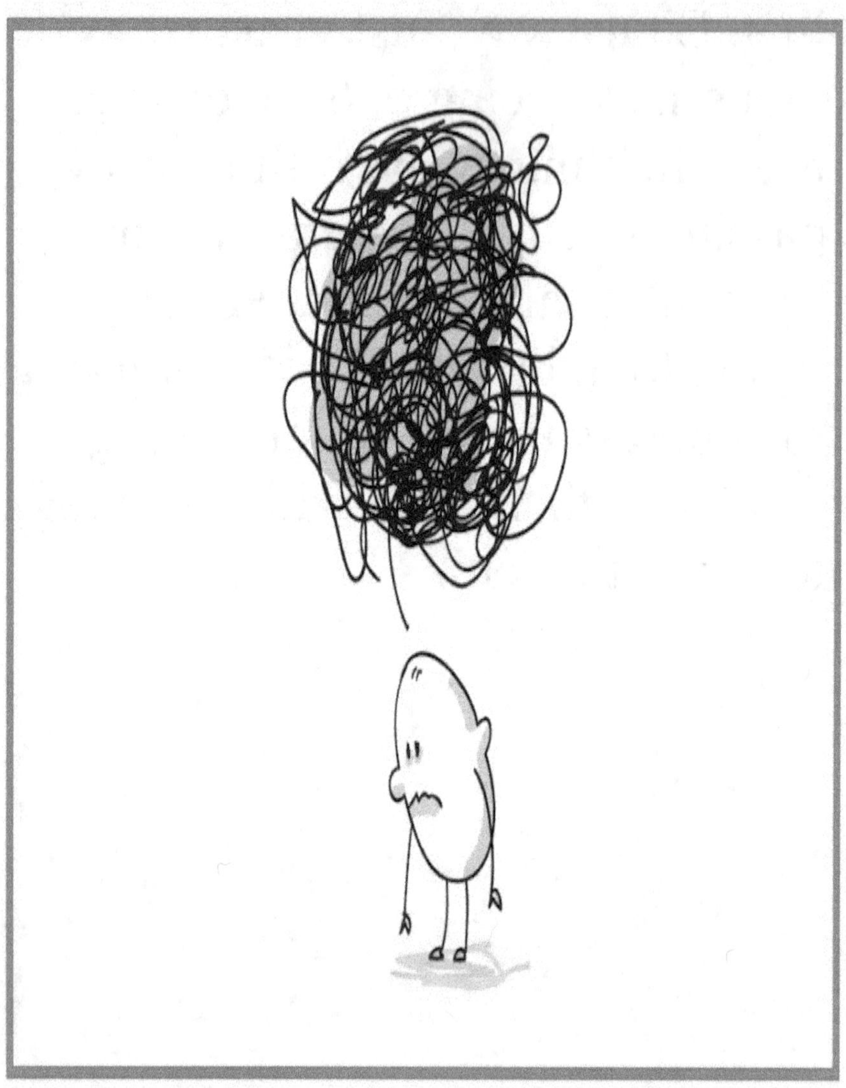

CHAPTER 4
HOW OVERTHINKING KILLS. THE CREATIVE PROCESS AND THE WAYS TO PREVENT IT

HOW OVERTHINKING KILLS

When we overthink something, we allow the creative, problem-solving half of our brain to take over and we lose any sense of rational judgment. The more decisions we make in order to attain a conclusion or end goal, the more prone we are to experience "decision fatigue."

But when you overthink, your mind goes in circles and you find yourself caught in backward, unable to move forward. Furthermore, you begin to have weird beliefs that completely contradict one another.

THE WAYS TO PREVENT IT

Here are 8 steps to help you stop overthinking.

1. Change The Story You Tell Yourself

I always used to say out loud: "I can never be on time. I'm not a morning person. I can't commit to anything." Well, guess what? I was never on time for meetings, I was always grumpy in the mornings and I couldn't commit to anything—a job, a relationship, or a side project.

That's because we are the stories we tell ourselves.

What you repeatedly say to yourself—and how you repeatedly describe yourself—is what you come to believe and be. Everything we do and experience stems from our identity and underlying set of beliefs.

The question is then, does the story you tell yourself empower you or hold you back?

Thoughts like "I'm an over-thinker" "I always worry because I have so much on my mind" or "I'm not really good with making decisions and I overthink everything" do you more harm than good.

If this is the story you tell yourself, you need to stop immediately because it's stripping away your power.

Instead, do this:

Identify those limiting beliefs and make a conscious effort to stop yourself whenever you catch yourself voicing them. Immediately replace those negative narratives with positive, empowering thoughts: "I am in charge of my emotions", "I think clearly" and, "I'm a decision-maker."

This is how you change your self-perception and begin to win back your power.

2. Let Go of The Past

Overthinkers often ruminate about the past.

When they do, they're exerting energy on the "what if" "I wish" and "I should have"… But that energy is removing them from the present moment.

The past cannot be changed—but you can change the lessons, meanings, and perspectives you extract from it.

When you accept the past for what it was, you relieve yourself from its weight. You will then free your mind from the burdens, mistakes, or grudges of the past that stop you from taking action in the present.

Learning to let go of the past is something we must constantly work on because it's so easy to slip back into the habit of rumination. This is essential as it clears up the mental space that was occupied by overthinking it.

3. Stop Your Thoughts in The Moment and Practice Being Present

In the heat of overthinking, stop and say:

"No. I'm not going to have these thoughts right now. I'm not going to give in."

Bring your attention to where you are here and now.

Breathe. Focus. Where are you? What do you feel? What's on your mind? What's stressing you out?

Open your journal and write down your thoughts. Research shows that the habit of writing what we feel helps us with metacognitive thinking.

Metacognition is "thinking about one's thinking", or in simpler terms, it's our "awareness of our own thoughts." That's why you become more aware of your thoughts and what they're trying to tell you when you write them down.

The goal is to become more aware and remove yourself from the "being" of your thoughts. You want to observe your thoughts so you can understand what they are and *why* you're feeling them.

Being present isn't easy. It requires practice. But whenever you notice your mind ruminating about the past or wandering into the future, try to bring it back to this moment and think:

"The past doesn't matter. The future is out of my reach. All I have in my control is this present moment. So I will stop thinking about the past or the present. I will only think about the here and now."

Daily rituals like journaling, meditation, or writing one line per day help you retain control over your mind so that you can stay in the present and practice living in the moment. They also reduce stress, improve focus, and increase self-awareness.

This practice will be difficult in the beginning, but as with anything, in due time, it will begin to transform your life and come more naturally. Above all, higher awareness will help you reduce your overthinking.

4. Focus on What You Can Control

"When you find yourself worrying, take a minute to examine the things you have control over."

First, acknowledge what's on your mind. Second, take a step back and broaden your perspective. Ask yourself: "What can I control?"

"Focusing exclusively on what is in our power magnifies and enhances our power."—Ryan Holiday

If you're struggling financially and ruminating about how you're going to pay the bills—that doesn't help. What helps is looking at your expenses and thinking 'What can I cut or eliminate from my bills?' Then ask 'What other revenue streams can I create?' This is how you shift your attention from what you can't control, to what you can.

5. Identify Your Fears

Very often, it's the irrational fears that arise in our minds that lead to overthinking.

We fear what others might think, we fear making a mistake, and we fear not being good enough to succeed. Living in that fear will tangle us in a well of indecision.

Roman Stoic and Philosopher Seneca said:

"We suffer more often in imagination than in reality."

Fear, which often stems from the imagination of "what might be", contributes to your overthinking. And one of the best strategies to beat fear is to simply take action. Take a small step in the direction of your fear and see what happens. The moment you take action is the moment you win a battle with your overthinking. Win more battles with more action.

As Napoleon Hill, author of Think and Grow Rich, writes:

"Fear can be effectively cured by forced repetition of acts of courage."

When I'm overwhelmed within indecision, I usually ask myself: "what's the worse that could happen?"

And when I've figured out what that would be, I spend some time thinking of a contingency plan. This gives me the confidence to take the action I need and note be afraid of it.

6. Write Down (or Openly Share) Solutions (Not Problems)

"Energy flows where attention goes."

To stop overthinking, you must address the problems at hand. When you feel overwhelmed, take some time to write down all your thoughts in your head, but then shift your attention to the solutions.

Give your power and energy to solutions.

The problems and thoughts you list are the weeds creating stress and anxiety.

After surfacing them on paper, or voicing them to a friend, now's the time to brainstorm solutions.

Is your work causing you stress? Okay good. Now, what changes can you make to reduce it? Is your stagnation in life causing you anxiety? Ok good. What steps can you take to get more clarity on the goals you need to pursue?

Being open and honest about your thoughts and sharing them with someone you trust can offer a new "out of the box" perspective. Sometimes, we just need to "vent"—but don't make this a habitual go-to escape.

I always say to friends:

"I'm here if you need me. But come to me with solutions, not problems."

If you arrive with (at least) one solution, that means you've taken the time to think and swim through your thoughts. Coming with problems means you're at square zero.

Learn to manage and regulate your emotions, thoughts, and mind. You can build the mental strength for it.

Get your thoughts out of your head so you can raise your awareness of them and observe them. Then shift your attention to the solutions you can create to relieve them.

7. Make The Decision to Become a Person of Action

There are two ideas at play here: making a decision and taking action.

One of the challenges of overthinking is that you get lost in the circus inside your head—which then leads you to indecision. This is the worst place to be in. Because if you get stuck in the same place, spinning around in the carousel of your thoughts, forward movement eludes you.

What you need to do is practice making decisions and sticking with them.

Point the arrow and pull the trigger.

And do this for the smallest of decisions.

Chocolate or vanilla? 3–2–1 Choose! Order in or cook dinner> 3–2–1 Choose!

Through the practice of being decisive, you automatically become a person of action. Because action stems from a decision—and the latter comes from you.

8. Manage Your Stress: Move, Unplug, Spend Time in Nature

Study some published in Psychological Science revealed that the brain becomes both calmer and sharper after a person spends time in a quiet setting close to nature. Other research also concludes that walking in green spaces puts the brain in a meditative state.

Even a walk in a 5-minute walk in the park can have an immediate calming effect on the mind.

Whenever you feel overwhelmed with thoughts, one of these three things can help you clear your head:

1. A walk in nature (or a nearby park).

2. Exercise. It is scientifically proven to be an instant mood booster and stress-reducer. Sweating out your thoughts helps you think clearly.

3. Unplugging from all digital devices for a few hours.

TWO MAIN FACTORS CONTRIBUTE TO OVERTHINKING:

- Behavior (the ways we think and act).
- Stress

Bahavior: The fundamental cause of overthinking is the way a person thinks and acts.

we learn the majority of our behaviors before the age of eight, and those behaviors are significantly impacted by those who raise us throughout our formative years. As a result, the environment we grow up in, as well as our parents' parenting approaches, have a significant impact on how we behave as adults.

With that in mind, here are some of the numerous reasons why humans overthink. Over thinkers in general:

Are quite analytical.
Have IQs that are greater than the average.
Were frequently reared by overly critical parents.
Growing up, you may have witnessed a horrific occurrence or events.
Growing up, you may have been subjected to abuse (physical, psychological, emotional, sexual, or spiritual).

1. Stress

Stress negatively affects brain function in important ways that affect critical thinking. For instance, stress hampers the areas of the brain responsible for critical thinking (the cortex). As stress increases, suppression of the cortex increases.

But that's not all. Stress also increases the activity in the fear center of the brain , which causes an increase in thought generation. This increased thought generation takes on a more dire tone due to the fear center's heightened influence.

Moreover, the cortex is also responsible for applying the "anxiety brake" that stops anxious thinking. When the cortex is suppressed and the fear center is more active, we have a much more difficult time shutting off anxious thinking.

As such, stress, and more importantly, chronic stress, is the most common cause of incessant mind chatter with a reduced ability to rationalize and shut it off.

Furthermore, problem-solving causes mental exertion, which also stresses the body.[8] As mental exertion increases, stress increases, incessant mind-chatter increases, and our ability to think clearly and critically decreases.

10 STEPS TO STOP OVERTHINKING

1. Awareness

To change a behavior, we first have to become aware of the behavior. So, the first step in making healthy behavioral changes is to become aware of when you are overthinking.

You can do this by paying attention to your thoughts and life and making a note of every time you catch yourself overthinking. As your awareness of overthinking becomes more apparent, you are then prepared to begin the change process.

Awareness will alert you to common situations and circumstances where you overthink. When those situations and circumstances arise, they will alert you to pay attention to what you are thinking.

Awareness is the first step in making behavior.

2. Write out what you are overthinking about

Too often we dwell on issues without clearly articulating what we're overthinking about. Then, we run in thought circles without a definite direction.

Writing out what you are overthinking about, and then clearly identifying the problem you are concerning yourself with can bring clarity that can help with problem-solving.

Sometimes, overthinking isn't about problem-solving but ruminating about something that is bothering you. Either way, clearly identifying what you are overthinking can help bring it to a successful resolution.

3. Research your options

Many people overthink based on the options they think they have without knowing all of the options that are truly available. Take time and research what options are realistic and available, rather than limiting yourself to just the ones you initially think are available.

4. Write out your options

Once you have your options, write them out. Writing out your options solidifies them, making decision-making easier and less about thinking and ruminating.

5. Set a time limit for your problem-solving

Setting a time limit gives you a concrete time frame to work with. Leaving the decision-making process open-ended sets you up for unlimited overthinking.

This time limit can be a few hours for some problems and up to several days for more complicated problems. Nevertheless, you need to set a time limit that you can work toward. The goal is, once you reach the end of that time limit, you want to have made your final decision.

Do your best to adhere to that time limit. Continually changing the time limit encourages overthinking.

6. Give yourself a break from the problem

Many people try to come up with a decision quickly so that they can move on to other things. They believe that if they think enough, and consecutively, they can solve the problem and move on to the next one. Trying to solve a problem in one stretch, however, doesn't give you time to reflect with a fresh mind and attitude.

It's recommended to build in some time away from the problem so you can reflect on it with fresh thinking to ensure your decision is sound. Time away can be a few hours for less important decisions, or up to a week or more for more important decisions.

Also, when you take a break, be sure to set a specific time to revisit the problem. That way, if your mind wanders back to the problem during your break, you can reassure yourself that you are working on it and will complete the process at that specific time.

Knowing that you intend to solve the problem at a specific time makes it easier to dismiss meandering thoughts when they intrude on your time away from the problem.

7. Give yourself permission to take time away

While it's great to take time away from decision-making, you have to hold yourself accountable to that decision so that you can come back to it with a fresh mind. You can accomplish this by giving yourself permission to take time away from your decision-making.

Giving yourself permission is saying, "It's good to stop thinking about this so that I can revisit it with a fresh perspective. Therefore, I'm giving myself permission to ignore it for now knowing I will revisit it later."

Then, whenever your mind cycles back to the problem during that away time, you can say, "No, I'm not focusing on that now. I've given myself permission to ignore it until later. I will revisit it at the specified time. I'm not being irresponsible."

Giving yourself permission can make it easier to ignore the problem for the short term, especially when you know you will revisit it at a predetermined time in the future.

8. Hold yourself accountable with your time away

Okay, you've given yourself permission to ignore the problem until the predetermined time. That's great! But when your thoughts cycle back to the problem, you have to hold yourself accountable for not revisiting it until the predetermined time.

You can do that by saying to yourself, "No, I'm not resuming this problem-solving until the predetermined time.

Taking a break from it is an important part of the overall problem-solving process. I'm not going to sabotage it by re-engaging too soon. I have permission to take a break and I'm going to take it."

Also, remind yourself taking a break reduces stress, which can benefit the decision-making process (not to mention your overall health).

9. Come up with a final decision during the predetermined revisit time

Be sure to set a time limit on this revisit time. It can be whatever you think is appropriate to arrive at a good decision. For instance, some problems require a revisit time of only 10 to 15 minutes. Others might take an hour or so. Others might require an entire day.

Whatever the problem, set an appropriate time limit to arrive at a final decision. Then, it's your goal to come up with a final decision during this predetermined revisit time.

10. Hold yourself accountable for your decision and deliberately "put a pin" in the problem

Once you've reached the end of your time limit and have made a decision, hold yourself accountable to that decision and stop the thinking process.

You can view this final decision as being completed with no wiggle room. Whenever your mind wants to cycle back and revisit your decision, you need to stop and remind yourself that the decision-making process is completed. You've done your best, and the results will be what they will be.

If the results aren't producing the desired outcome, you can always revisit the problem and change course if need be later on after you've given your decision suitable time to have an effect.

Following the above-mentioned process can significantly reduce overthinking…as long as you hold yourself accountable to it. If accountability is a skill you have to develop, so be it. Working at stopping overthinking is a good way to develop that skill.

Since we are all in charge of the thoughts we think, all of us can learn the ability to "contain," which means limiting behavior (the ways we think and act). We all have the ability to direct our thoughts so there is nothing holding us back other than habit and effort.